IMAGES
of Wales

NEWPORT
EAST OF THE RIVER

NEWPORT
TRANSPORTER BRIDGE
opened by
Rt HON. VISCOUNT TREDEGAR,
September 12th, 1906.

The front cover of a booklet commemorating the opening of the Transporter Bridge by Viscount Tredegar in 1906. It had become clear that a second river crossing was needed at the turn of the century to cope with the flow of traffic and access to the southern end of Newport. The town's population had increased greatly and with the development on the east side of the river and the large workforce now employed at Lysaght's Orb Steelworks, a Transporter Bridge was decided upon. The other options of ferry, high level bridge and swing bridge were not considered as viable as the Transporter Bridge, due to the wide and fast-flowing Usk which has one of the greatest tidal ranges in the world.

IMAGES
of Wales

NEWPORT
EAST OF THE RIVER

Compiled by
Rachael Anderton
from the collections of
Newport Museum and Art Gallery

Newport
COUNTY BOROUGH
BWRDEISTREF SIROL
Casnewydd

TEMPUS

First published 2002
Reprinted 2004

Tempus Publishing Limited
The Mill, Brimscombe Port,
Stroud, Gloucestershire, GL5 2QG
www.tempus-publishing.com

British Library Cataloguing in Publication Data.
A catalogue record for this book is available from the British Library.

ISBN 0 7524 2462 9

Typesetting and origination by Tempus Publishing Limited.
Printed in Great Britain.

For my family

George Street Bridge, after it had been opened in 1964, showing Llanwern Steelworks in the
background.

Contents

Ruby Loftus screwing a breech-ring for an anti-aircraft gun in the Royal Ordnance Factory at Newport in 1943. A painting of this scene by Dame Laura Knight is part of the Imperial War Museum collections.

A general view of the fitting section in the Royal Ordnance Factory at Newport during the Second World War.

Introduction

In 1995 Newport Museum and Art Gallery published *Newport West of the River*, a book of around 200 photographs from the Local History collections, compiled by Alex Dawson, Keeper of Human History. This is the second volume, a book of photographs showing life on the east side of the River Usk, all selected from the vast number in the Museum and Art Gallery collections.

While it is very similar in style to the first publication, there are some different aspects which we hope will complement both volumes. In this book there is a chapter on bridges, to show the importance of the links between the east and west side of the river. We have also included a chapter on urban development, with photographs of areas of the east side of Newport that have changed dramatically over the years. It is hoped these will be of considerable interest to readers.

The photographic collections of Newport Museum and Art Gallery are made up from generous donations by people in Newport and reflect the history of the town through their eyes. It is essentially their collection and we hope that this book will bring the past of the east side of Newport to life.

Rachael Anderton
Newport Museum and Art Gallery
November 2001

A map of Newport showing the development of the east side, *c.* 1900.

One
Bridges

The older Town Road Bridge from the east side before it was dismantled in 1927.

The first railway bridge in Newport. The bridge was designed by Robert Brunel, having an entire span of 700ft from bank to bank, with eleven arches, 50ft each and a ground centre span of 100ft. The cost was more than £20,000.

The first railway bridge across the River Usk on fire in 1848. The Great Western Railway began work in 1846 on both sides of the river. The timber bridge was nearly completed in 1848 when it was destroyed by fire. Within six minutes of the first flame igniting, the whole bridge was aflame. The fire was thought to have been started by a workman who was using a heated rimer but did not have water nearby as required by safety regulations. The bridge was rebuilt immediately after the fire and the railway opened in 1850.

Road and railway bridges link the east and west banks of the River Usk.

A view from the east side of the river of the railway bridge with the bow arch construction.

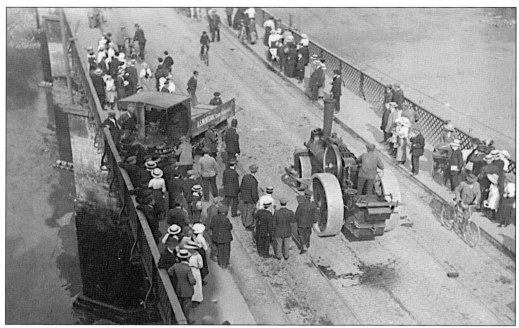

An accident on the Town Bridge, 29 June 1914, caused by the breaking of the steering gear in the lorry. The traction engine appears to be preparing to remove the lorry.

In 1927 the new Town Bridge was completed and the old bridge was dismantled. Wooden structures were built under the arches to hold them up and prevent stones from falling into the river as the work of demolition progressed.

The opening of the new Town Bridge in 1927. As Newport grew to the east of the River Usk, good communications across the river were vital to the development of the town.

The new Town Bridge decorated for the Coronation celebrations of George VI in 1937.

Perhaps the most easily recognized Newport landmark, the Transporter Bridge, was completed in 1906 and was designed by Ferdinand Arnodin. The bridge is seen here during construction, which lasted four years. No workers were killed and only minor injuries were sustained, which is even more remarkable after looking at this photograph and seeing the men working on the boom. The bridge cost £98,000 and, as a suspended ferry, it could be worked more easily and rapidly than a conventional ferry and would be safer from shipping hazards. A moving traveller attached to a gondola is pulled along by cables from a motor base. The height from ground level to the top of the towers is 73.7 metres while the span from the centre to the centre of the two towers is 196.6 metres.

The opening of the Transporter Bridge by Lord Tredegar on 12 September 1906.

COUNTY BOROUGH of NEWPORT

TRANSPORTER BRIDGE.

NOTICE IS HEREBY GIVEN

That on and after SUNDAY NEXT, the 1st DECEMBER, 1918, the TOLLS for the conveyance of Passengers, Animals, Vehicles, and Goods across the River Usk by means of the above Bridge, for each crossing, either way, will be as under :---

1. For every person ... ... **One penny**
   Books of 12 Tickets (not transferable) ... ... **Ninepence**

2. For every horse, mule, ass, ox, cow, bull, or head of cattle ... ... **Twopence**
   For every calf, pig, sheep, lamb, or other small animal ... ... **One penny**

3. For every unloaded vehicle weighing not more than one ton—
   a. If drawn by not more than one horse, ass or mule **Threepence**
   b. If drawn by more than one horse, ass or mule, for every horse, ass or mule beyond the first **Twopence**

4. For every loaded vehicle carrying not more than 1½ tons—
   a. If drawn by not more than one horse, ass or mule ... ... **Sixpence**
   b. If drawn by more than one horse, ass or mule, for every horse, ass or mule beyond the first **Twopence**

5. For every loaded vehicle carrying a load exceeding 1½ tons but not exceeding 2 tons ... ... **One Shilling**
   For every loaded vehicle carrying a load exceeding 2 tons but not exceeding 10 tons for every ton or part of a ton ... ... **One Shilling**
   For every horse, mule or ass drawing such vehicle ... ... **Twopence**

6. For every vehicle carrying a load exceeding 10 tons the Corporation may demand such sum as they may think fit.

7. For every hand truck unloaded ... ... **Twopence**
   For every hand truck carrying a load not exceeding 10 cwt. ... ... **Fourpence**
   For every hand truck carrying a load not exceeding 20 cwt. ... ... **Sixpence**
   For every hand truck carrying a load exceeding 20 cwt. For every 5 cwt. ... **Threepence**
   For every bicycle or velocipede ... ... **One Penny**

8. For every motor vehicle loaded or unloaded—
   a. If not exceeding 30 cwt. in weight ... ... **Fourpence**
   b. Exceeding 30 cwt. but not exceeding 40 cwt. ... ... **Eightpence**
   c. Exceeding 40 cwt. but not exceeding 50 cwt. ... ... **One shilling**
   d. Exceeding 50 cwt. but not exceeding 60 cwt. ... ... **Two shillings**
   e. Exceeding 60 cwt. but not exceeding 70 cwt. ... ... **Three shillings**
   f. Exceeding 70 cwt. but not exceeding 80 cwt. ... ... **Four shillings**
   g. Exceeding 80 cwt. but not exceeding 90 cwt. ... ... **Four shillings and Sixpence**
   h. Exceeding 90 cwt. but not exceeding 100 cwt. ... ... **Five shillings**
   i. For every motor vehicle exceeding 100 cwt. the Corporation may demand such sum as they think fit.

9. For every parcel—
   a. If not exceeding 1 cwt. ... ... **One penny**
   b. If exceeding 1 cwt. for every cwt. or part thereof ... ... **One penny**

By Order,

ALBERT A. NEWMAN,
Town Clerk.

Town Hall, Newport,
27th November, 1918.

W. JONES, PRINTER, 114 COMMERCIAL STREET, NEWPORT.

A list of tolls for the Transporter Bridge, issued in 1918. On the opening day 8,000 people paid the penny toll but, unfortunately, the bridge always ran at a loss. It was used less and less when the Alexandra Dock gave shipping access to the Bristol Channel and the George Street Bridge was built. The bridge was restored in the 1990s and reopened in 1995 with the addition of floodlighting. There is now a Visitor Centre in the old manager's office with an exhibition explaining the history of the bridge, a film and an interactive model.

Among the celebrity visitors to be photographed on the Transporter Bridge was the Duke of York, later King George VI, seen here on the gondola during a visit in 1924. The loose chain across the front and back of the gondola would cause concern for health and safety inspectors today. The Duke had stopped off at Newport for an informal visit on his way to Cardiff to watch

a Rugby International match. Less than twenty transporter bridges were built in the world, between 1893 and 1916. Only six are thought to remain, three of them in Great Britain. The first transporter bridge was built near Bilbao in Spain, also designed by Ferdinand Arnodin. The bridge is still in use today.

George Street Bridge during construction in December 1963.

Aerial view of the new George Street Bridge, 1971. When first opened in 1964 the bridge did much to relieve traffic congestion in the town centre which sometimes caused queues of two miles around the Newport Bridge area. A special Act of Parliament was needed to construct a bridge over a navigable waterway and the Newport Corporation Act 1961 for the construction of George Street Bridge was probably the last local Act for this purpose. Construction work began on the bridge in 1962 and apparently cost less than the tender price of £985,160.

Two
Streets and Buildings

St Julian's House, demolished in 1980 after being left derelict since the 1960s. In 1800, apart from St Julian's House and a few other farm buildings, there were no other buildings in the area now known as Maindee. The house was extensively rebuilt in 1880. It was at one time the residence of Lord Herbert of Cherbury who was a well-known writer and prominent man at the court of Queen Elizabeth I. The house then passed to his son Richard, Lord Herbert of Cherbury who was Governor of Newport Castle in 1645. It was then sold to Joseph Firbank Esq., a railway contractor, High Sheriff of Monmouthshire, and JP for the County Borough of Newport and County of Monmouth.

LORD HERBERT of CHERBURY.

Engraved by Silvester Harding from an original Picture by Larting in the Collection of the Revd. Mr. Lucy Charlcott, Warwickshire

An engraving of Lord Herbert of Cherbury whose family arms were kept above the original doorway in the rebuilt house of 1880. St Julian's is named after the place of martyrdom of St Julius during the Roman occupation.

The garage of Albany Motors, coach and motor body builders, who were based at St Julian's House in the late 1950s.

The sale catalogue for The Maindee in 1874. This became the property of Ebenezer Lewis, JP, but he spent a lot of his older years at Weston before his death in 1901. The house then remained empty until it was bought by the Cardiff Estate Agency which demolished it in 1908 in order to build new houses.

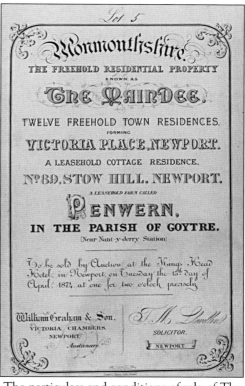

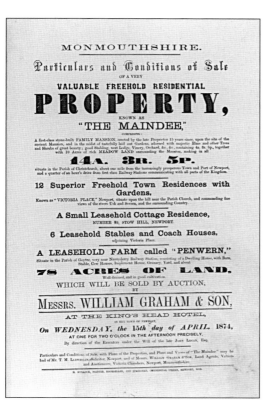

The particulars and conditions of sale of The Maindee: just one share of the Maindee estate which had been sold in the mid-nineteenth century to four people. At that time the railway and canal engineering contractor John Logan bought the share which included the run-down mansion, The Maindee. He built a new house and kept his prize-winning Shorthorn herd on the rest of the land. The rest of the estate including Eve's Well, Fair Oak and Pen Y Lan farms was sold to another railway and canal engineering contractor, James Rennie, a land agent, William Graham, and a solicitor, Henry Farr. The Fair Oak farmlands had been sold to Newport Freehold Land Society. Another mansion was built by James Rennie and his estate became known as Maindee Park, which was sold in 1875 to George Inglis Jones of Abergavenny. The latter allowed his brother to build a large house in the grounds which became known as Maindee Hall. The house, which had fifteen rooms on the ground floor, ten on the first floor and eight on the second, was eventually converted into flats in the 1920s.

Maindee Square, a hive of activity in the 1900s.

Maindee Square, 1959.

Maindee Square, with a view of Maindee Cinema, 1959.

Maindee Square after the installation of the fountain and flower beds.

The Cenotaph in Clarence Place was built in 1923. In this wintry scene a bus struggles to make headway up Chepstow Road.

An unseasonable snow storm hits Newport on April Fool's Day, 1922. The tram seems to be still moving here on Corporation Road.

A view of Chepstow Road in the snow, 1 April 1922.

The top of Christchurch, looking down the lane. The damage caused by telegraph poles being blown over by a storm during the winter of 1916-1917 can be seen.

A view of the storm damage looking up the lane towards the house and Christchurch from the opposite angle to above.

Some women linger and contemplate the damage done after the storm, at the bottom of the narrow road leading towards Christchurch.

A group of men and a horse and cart stop for a photograph, as they clear up after the storm damage on the top of Christchurch Hill, by the old coaching house, during the winter of 1916-1917.

An ice-cream van caught in floods in Exeter Road, Maindee.

The corner of Caerleon Road and Chepstow Road before 1922. The Cenotaph was built where the kiosk stands in this picture.

A crowd gathers at the war memorial in Clarence Place, which has now replaced the kiosk in the previous image.

Clarence Place has been highly decorated here for the Coronation of King George VI in 1937. The tram services ended not long after, in September 1937.

Clarence Place during the 1950s with a view towards the junction of Caerleon Road and Chepstow Road.

Two boys outside No. 199 Caerleon Road, 1911. One of the boys later discovered that the woman he married had also lived in the same house at some point!

A view of Chepstow Road, c. 1910.

In the early 1900s the traffic scene was vastly different from today. Here a tram travels along Chepstow Road.

A view of a different stretch of Chepstow Road, with another tram travelling along the road.

A view of Corporation Road and the Coliseum Picture Theatre, in the early 1900s.

St Julian's Road with very few cars parked outside the houses, *c.* 1950. Note the old-style telephone box.

Morden Road, a hive of activity during the early 1900s.

Three
Agriculture

Wyndham Howells, a fisherman at Goldcliffe, seen here repairing a wire putcher for salmon putching. The high rise and fall of the River Severn means a huge amount of putchers can be submerged in 'ranks' of feasible length. This putcher, made of sea-resistant aluminium wire, is the modern style adopted at Goldcliff since 1952, rather than the traditional putcher made with staves and banding of specially grown willow.

Wyndham Howells, seen here with his bicycle. The right of fishing at Goldcliffe with the nearby lands of the Priory were given to Eton College when it was founded in the reign of Henry VI. Although the ownership changed, the ancient fishery continued into the twentieth century.

Wyndham Howells with his model of the putcher rank in 1983. Putchers were the rows of funnel-shaped baskets on the stout framework which is built across the main tidal flow. Fish were then trapped in the putchers on the following tide.

These kypes at Goldcliffe were for catching prawns.

Milking time for the cows at Lliswerry Farm in 1953. Lliswerry Farm was demolished in 1955.

These two young lads are standing in the Lliswerry Farm milk float in 1950. Until the 1950s, milk was still sold directly to the public by local farmers, sometimes even being measured out into customers' jugs from the churn, although standard bottles had been available since the 1920s.

Four
Work and Industry

Mendelssohn Davies, the owner at the Alexandra Pottery in Dudley Street, Newport, before 1939. 'Mendie' Davies owned his own corn and seed merchant business in Risca but was asked to take over the Alexandra Potteries by Lovell the confectioner who no longer wanted to run it.

George Ovey at Alexandra Pottery in Dudley Street before 1939. The business came to a halt when war started as the site was taken over by an ordnance factory. (See wartime chapter).

George Ovey alongside the kiln at Alexandra Pottery in Dudley Street. He came from Barnstaple to work for Mendie Davies in 1937 and was a traditional craftsman and potter. Under his guidance, the pottery started to produce a wide range of highly glazed coloured ware and was being modernized by the outbreak of war in 1939.

Freedom of the town being given to W.R. Lysaght in 1936, by the Mayor of Newport, Councillor W. Casey. Also included in the picture are the Mayoress of Newport, Alderman Frederick Phillips, JP, and Alderman Dr J. Lloyd Davies (both receiving the Freedom of Newport as well), Alderman C.T. Clissitt and Councillor J.R. Wardell. The managing director of Lysaght's Ltd, W.R. Lysaght, brought the Orb Works to Newport in 1898 and this eventually became the company's headquarters. During the 1930s, the steel sheet industry progressed rapidly, especially with the growth of the car industry. The move to Newport was prompted because of the advantages of the shipping facilities and closeness to the South Wales coalfields. The Lysaght family was connected with the Orb Works until the 1970s even though it was taken over by Guest, Keen & Nettlefords, who acquired controlling interests. It became part of the new steelworks at Port Talbot. Lysaght's Ltd was also a founder member of the Steel Company of Wales in 1947.

A group of Lysaght's employees gathered on 1 March 1943 to celebrate fifty years' service to the company. From left to right, back row: J. Bird, C. Griffiths, H. Spicer, C. W. Painter, A. Kitson, W. Roden, L. Davies, J.R. Williams, W. Lightwood, S. White, J.T. Blud, A. Lane, J. Lewis. Middle row: W. Mason, T. Slattery, S. Clarke, B. Phillips, W. Trickett, J. Jones, G. Bate, J.C. Mincher, W. Barklam, W. Clarke, J.P. Herrity, J. Carvell, H. Edwards, J.E. Richards, J. Mcloughlin. Front row: W. Oldfield, J. Hurford, B. Smith, T. Cording, H. Prigg, T. Halfpenny, E. Lamb, T. Summerhill, F.J. Pugh, B. Dalton, W. Taylor, J. Griffiths, J. Hayward.

Laying the foundation stone at the Lysaght Institute in 1928, which was built with the co-operation of employees and W.R. Lysaght Ltd. It provided good leisure facilities for the employees of Lysaght's and included a billiard room, a skittle alley, a public bar, a saloon lounge and many cloakrooms and washrooms.

The millmen in the Orb Works at No. 7 Mill. During the Second World War, at its peak, the Orb Works employed 3,600 people when they were involved in manufacturing cartridge brass of special quality for aircraft cannon shells. In 1901 there was a 3,000 strong workforce, many of whom came from Wolverhampton after the closure of the firm's works there in 1901. This number included 600 girls who also worked the three eight-hour shifts. At this time this was practically the only plant in the world making thin steel sheet and expanded from four mills to forty mills by 1913.

Poster of street works issued by the County Borough of Newport.

County Borough of Newport

PRIVATE STREET WORKS

in _____ Llanvair Rd (Part)

NOTICE IS HEREBY GIVEN that the Corporation are about to carry out Works of Private Street Improvement in the above-named street in accordance with Plans prepared by the Borough Engineer.

If any Owner of premises in the said street is desirous of carrying out any part of the works in front of such premises, he must, after giving notice of his intention, do so within **one month** from the date hereof, to the satisfaction of the Borough Engineer, as no allowance will be made by the Corporation in respect of any works which may be carried out by a frontager after the service of the Notice of the Provisional Apportionment.

Dated this 2nd. day of July 1910

Albert A. Newman
TOWN CLERK

County Borough of Newport.

PRIVATE STREET WORKS
IN
EVESWELL LANE.

To all whom it may concern.

WHEREAS Notice has been served upon the Corporation of the County Borough of Newport, in pursuance of the Newport (Monmouthshire) Corporation Act, 1889, that the Owner of certain premises shown in the Provisional Apportionment of the expenses of Private Street Works in the above-named Street, as liable to be charged with part of the expense of executing such works, objects to the proposals of the Corporation upon some or one of the grounds set forth in Section 88 of the Act,

AND WHEREAS application has been made to a Court of Summary Jurisdiction to appoint a time for determining the matter of such objection,

NOW, THEREFORE, notice is hereby given that such Court has appointed

Wednesday, the 13th August, 1913.
AT 12 O'CLOCK NOON,

at the TOWN HALL, in the said County Borough of Newport, as the time and place for determining such objection.

ALBERT A. NEWMAN,
TOWN CLERK.

Dated this 28th day of July, 1913.

GEORGE BELL, Printer, Stationer, and Lithographer, 13 Commercial Street, Newport.

Poster of street works issued by the County Borough of Newport.

The factory of F. James (Newport) Ltd on Corporation Road, who were distributors of Nunbetta products: canned goods, dried fruits, groceries, confectionery, paper, and bags and general sundries.

COUNTY BOROUGH OF NEWPORT.

PRIVATE STREET WORKS

IN

BERESFORD ROAD

AND

GRAFTON ROAD.

NOTICE IS HEREBY GIVEN, that in pursuance of the Newport (Monmouthshire) Corporation Act. 1889, the Corporation of the County Borough of Newport, acting by the Town Council, at a Meeting held on Tuesday, the 12th day of April. 1904, duly passed the following resolution, viz :

"That the respective specifications, plans and sections, estimates and provisional apportionments, prepared by the Borough Engineer, for private street works in Beresford Road and Grafton Road now submitted, in which apportionments regard is had to the amount and value of work already done by the owners or occupiers of premises fronting, adjoining, or abutting on the said respective streets, be approved."

And notice is hereby further given that, during one month from the date of the first publication hereof, the said specifications, plans and sections, estimates and provisional apportionments (or copies thereof certified by the Engineer), will be kept deposited at the offices of the Corporation (Engineer's Department), at the Town Hall, Newport, and will be open for inspection at all reasonable times.

Dated this 13th day of April, 1904.

ALBERT A. NEWMAN,

Poster of street works issued by the County Borough of Newport.

Mr Jack Ricketts, fitter, and Mr Bert Pugh, an ex-bus driver who was also fitter's mate. They are standing alongside a bus which was the first of the Daimler No 150s fitted with an experimental type clutch (centrifugal) because it was unsuitable for hills. Workers at Stewart and Lloyds would have used the Corporation Road route to and from work.

Mr Jack Ricketts, fitter, and Mr Joe Hards changing a saw blade on the hot saws section of the mills in Stewart and Lloyds Steel Tube Works, Corporation Road, during the 1960s. Stewart and Lloyds had started out as the British Mannesmann Tube Company's works in 1914, specializing in the large-scale production of steel tubes. It closed in 1974.

Llanwern Steelworks from the air in 1985. The Spencer Works as it was first known, named after the Managing Director of Richard, Thomas and Baldwins Ltd, was officially opened in 1962 by HM the Queen. Construction had begun in 1960. The site was chosen because of its closeness to Newport Docks for imports and exports, and the direct railway links with London and the Midlands – the two main market areas for steel sheet in Great Britain. It could also supply steel to the Ebbw Vale Steelworks. Spencer Works aimed to produce large amounts of sheet steel for export mainly for the car industry.

Another aerial view of Llanwern Steelworks, 1985. The plant was one of the most modern in the world when it was first opened. It was necessary to fill the site chosen for the construction as the land was so marshy and below sea level; consequently 9 million cubic yards of fill was used to raise the level of the site.

Uskmouth Power Station during construction. The original works of the Newport Electricity Undertaking started in 1895 in Llanarth Street, but demand for lighting and traction purposes grew so much that a new East Power Station was built in Corporation Road seven years later. For its time, the station was equipped with the most up-to-date plant, machinery and appliances for the modern production of electricity. In 1937, the Newport Electricity Undertaking had 24,790 consumers and had opened a new showroom in High Street with displays and demonstrations of electrical appliances.

The main building of Uskmouth Power Station, 1985. By 1946, the demand for electricity had grown so great that Newport Corporation proposed to the Central Electricity Board the construction of a new power station at the mouth of the River Usk. The area within Nash had been scheduled for industrial development and had good water supplies for cooling purposes, good railway connections to the South Wales coalfields and land available for ash deposit. Work began in 1948 under the direction of the recently formed British Electricity Authority. In 1957 work started on a second B station which was opened in 1963.

Aerial view of Uskmouth Power Station, 1985.

Five
Transport and Shipping

A paddle steamer at the landing stage near Newport Bridge in 1907.

The River Usk and its shipping have always been a mainstay of transportation in Newport. Here the paddle steamer *Glen Avon* is shown at the landing stage on the east bank in the early 1900s. This picture, taken from the upper floors of the market building on the west side of the river, clearly shows the familiar dome of the Technical College in the background. The *Glen Avon* was one of Campbell's pleasure steamers, a Bristol company founded in 1888 which operated its ships in the Bristol channel for ninety-two years. They called regularly at Newport, berthing at Rodney Parade just below Town Bridge. The last Campbell's boat to leave this landing stage departed in September 1956. As cars and the Severn Bridge were used more, fuel and maintenance costs became too much and the sailings in the Bristol Channel ceased at the end of the 1979 season.

Excursion traffic was very popular. Here Newport police are off to Minehead for their annual outing in 1908, as guests of the Watch Committee.

The Great Western Railway used a broad gauge rail track, wider than most other companies. Here the approaches to the station, looking east, are seen in the 1880s. The wagon on the right centre is on a small turntable to manoeuvre from the station yard to the main line.

The Grid Iron sweeper at work below Town Bridge. This structure was needed to keep ships upright in the large rise and fall of tidal water levels.

The railway strike of 1911 brought the troops out in East Newport. There were railway and coal strikes in South Wales during 1911-1912 despite it being a time of prosperity for the rail companies. In South Wales some railwaymen were being sent from Newport to London, allegedly to take the place of trade unionists, and as a result of this a mass meeting was called at the Tradesman Hall to decide what action should be taken. All Newport railway workers ceased work on Thursday 18 August and held a mass meeting at Pill Park, demanding better working conditions and an increase in wages as there had not been an increase for the previous thirteen years. The strike ended on 21 August and an agreement was made that all men who had been on strike would be reinstated: there would be a special Commission of Inquiry into the strike and into all the grievances of the workers.

There were dramatic scenes as a result of the railway strike at Maindee Junction as these policemen gathered at the East Usk Road to guard the signal box on 19 August 1911. A large crowd, at times at least 1,000 people, had gathered and jeered at drivers and firemen on passing trains to try and get them to join them in the strike. They were trying to get the signalmen to join them in the strike. At about 2 a.m. one man even attempted to get in the signal box, but was stopped by police, after which the crowd was dispersed.

A horse-drawn tram at the corner of Somerset Road in the early 1900s, with Mr Frank Bubb as the driver in the front. The horse-drawn tram service to Somerset Road opened in 1899. The first horse-drawn trams started in February 1875 and 1,084 passengers used the first two trams on the day after the official opening. Notice the pole for the telephone wires – the first Newport telephone exchange was opened in 1880.

The electric tramway came to Newport on 9 April 1903 at 2 p.m. and ran between Corporation Road (Lysaght's Works) and Pillgwenlly (the end of Commercial Road), via Clarence Place, High Street and Commercial Street. The service shown here was from Corporation Road to Pill. Along the route, crowds gathered to watch the first official electric tram journey and a large crowd watched the opening ceremony at the Corporation Road terminus.

Water covers the road at Maindee Railway bridge, but does not stop the buses and cars making their way through.

Some cars are stranded in flood water on the road at Maindee Railway bridge, while the one car does try to splash through.

Caerleon Road, the section known as 'the dip' and now the M4 access roundabout.

Motor traffic was not without its problems. Here a car at Five Lanes on Chepstow Road near Caerwent has mounted the kerb and struck a watchman's box. According to the press report, a woman was injured in the accident.

Six
Wartime

Members of the National Reserve drilling at Lysaght's Sports Ground in 1914.

The 1st Monmouthshire Regiment on a church parade in Maindee in October 1914.

Members of the Newport Athletic Club who were the first batch of recruits for the First World War in 1914.

A sugar ticket from the First World War for a retailer in Chepstow Road.

W. a 84

RETAILER'S SUGAR TICKET.

This Ticket is issued under the authority of the Food Controller by:—
_____
(*Retailer's Name and Address, written or rubber-stamped.*)

G. P. SIMMONDS
Chepstow Road,
NEWPORT.

in respect of the person named in Part A on the back, being a member of the household of:—
(*Householder's Name*) ....*Edmund Webb*..........
and must be produced to the Retailer upon every purchase of sugar in respect of that person.

NOTE.—The space above for the householder's name and Part A on the back must be filled up immediately upon the issue of this Ticket, and in any case before it is produced to the Retailer.

TRANSFER ON REMOVAL, Etc.

If the person named on the back removes altogether or ceases to be a member of the above-mentioned household, Part B on the back should be filled up and the Ticket should then be taken to a Post Office.

X 2360. W4645. 10,000m. 11/17. Drayton Mill. (E. 2033) F. 22.

Many large houses were used as hospitals or convalescent homes during both world wars. Here are some of the staff and patients at Beechwood House during the First World War.

Newport's First World War souvenir being cut up for scrap in 1937 after standing in a garden in Chepstow Road.

The Home Guard gave valuable service during the Second World War. Here are some of the Maindee Home Guard.

A programme for an ARP Wardens' dinner and social evening at Christchurch School, 15 February 1946, at 7 p.m.

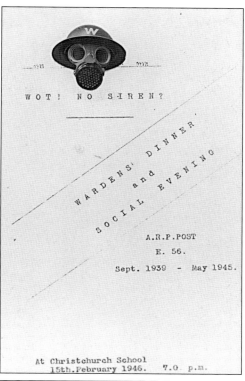

WOT! NO SIREN?

WARDENS' DINNER
and
SOCIAL EVENING

A.R.P. POST

E. 56.

Sept. 1939 - May 1945.

At Christchurch School
15th. February 1946.   7.0. p.m.

Mayor Wardell lays a wreath at the Cenotaph service of 1939. The Second World War had just started.

The Auxiliary Fire Service hold their first exercise in 1939/40 as part of Newport's air-raid precautions during the war. Here they are fixing trailer pumps at Brickworks Pond, St Julian's, in order to pump out water.

The Auxiliary Fire Service continued to practise at Brickworks Pond, St. Julian's during the Second World War.

A cheerful group of women workers at the Royal Ordnance Factory in Wednesbury Street during the Second World War – the site was formerly the Alexandra Pottery. (See the Work and Industry chapter.)

A general view of the fitting section in the Royal Ordnance Factory at Newport during the Second World War.

At the same factory, it seems lunch times were very energetic, with the women workers involved in a tug-of-war. The factory building in the background has its windows blacked out. From left to right: -?-, -?-, Muriel Swain, Eileen Beardsmore, Mrs Irene Williams,-?-, -?-.

A photograph of the military medal which was awarded to Gwyn Jones, who was a resident of Balmoral Road on the east side of the river. At the age of eighteen, Gwyn Jones was the first member of the Home Guard and the only civilian to win a Military Medal for his actions during a bomb raid on the night of 12/13 July 1940. Volunteer Jones was guarding a vital point (Whiteheads Iron and Steel Works at Newport Docks) when the post was bombed and one man was killed and another injured. When Gwyn Jones heard the cries of the wounded man, he left his safe shelter and carried the man on his back to safety, despite the danger of falling debris around him. The official report said, 'Volunteer Jones carried out his task with complete disregard to his own safety. His courageous behaviour set a fine example to all those concerned.'

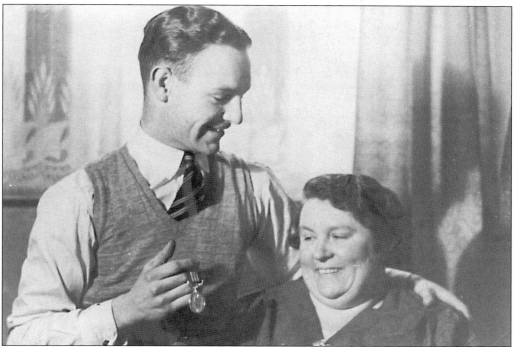

Gwyn Jones and his mother with his military medal. He received many letters of congratulations for his brave act, including one from the wife of the man who died in the incident and a telegram from Lord Tredegar. Gwyn Jones, born in Swansea, was the elder son of Mr J.R. Jones, a furnace man, and Mrs Jones, of No. 78 Balmoral Road, Newport. He lived in Newport from the age of five and attended Eveswell School and Hatherleigh Central School. He had an interest in athletics and was Victor Ludorum at Newport Central School for Sports in 1936. He won swimming and running medals and joined Newport Athletics Club, taking part in some of Monmouthshire's principal sports meetings.

A group celebrating VE Day at Emmanuel Church Hall in Maindee, 1945.

The VE Day party inside Emmanuel Church, London Street, in 1945. From left to right, front row: Robbie Hurd, Billy Harry, John Simpson, Margaret Simpson (Little Red Riding Hood).

Seven
Special Events

In the early part of the last century, the Newport police regularly held inspection parades at the Newport Athletic Club Ground. This view shows the 1900 parade. The Newport police force was established in 1840, although in 1838 the Town Council had employed men from the Bristol police force for 12 shillings a week, with a truncheon and cutlass included.

Mr J. Lawrence MP for Newport, Monmouth Borough, the Sheriff of London and Dr F. Rutherford Harris, MP for Newport (October 1900 to March 1901), arriving for a grand reception at Newport after the general election, May 1901, at the junction of Caerleon Road and Clarence Place.

The Carnegie Library was opened in Corporation Road in 1907. It was named after Andrew Carnegie, who had made a gift of the building as part of the 90 per cent of his fortune which he contributed to educational and arts facilities, with a real emphasis on libraries. A reading room was first opened in 1870 in a building which had previously been a Diocesan School and the Newport Mechanics' Institute, followed by a Lending Library in February 1871. In 1882 Mayor Thomas Beynon, who as a member of the council had advocated the provision of a library, opened the new Central Library in Dock Street, which had been built on ground given by Lord Tredegar. Branch libraries were opened after the initial success of the Lending Library Service in Dock Street. In 1871 27,922 books were borrowed by the people of Newport.

MONSTER FETE & GALA

To be held in Fields near the ROYAL OAK, CHEPSTOW ROAD. 1027

On THURSDAY, August 28th, 1919.

Pony and Galloway Races.

SPORTS, &c., (BY THE PILL HARRIERS.)

Proceeds divided between St. Dunstan's After Care Fund and Christchurch Public War Memorial	Madame Ada Thomas' Juvenile Dancers. FANCY DRESS CARNIVAL (for Children under 14,) And numerous EXTRAORDINARY ATTRACTIONS! A Prize will be given for Lucky Number Ticket, by Messrs. STYLE and MANTLE, High Street, Newport.
	BAND. REFRESHMENTS. DANCING.

ADULT'S TICKET, 1/-.   -:o:-   Gates open at 2 p.m.

An advertisement for a 'Monster' fête and gala to be held in the fields near the Royal Oak on Chepstow Road in August 1919 which was to include a fancy dress carnival and Madame Ada Thomas' Juvenile Dancers. The proceeds went to St Dunstan's After Care Fund and Christchurch Public War Memorial.

The Cenotaph in Clarence Place has seen many ceremonies. Here buglers from the 1st Rifle battalion of the Monmouthshire Regiment play the *Last Post* at a memorial service in 1934 to mark Armistice Day.

The Sea Cadets provide a Guard of Honour at a wet Armistice service.

The programme for the fair and pageant at Maindee Hall in 1935 held to help the Waifs and Strays Society. The society's local home was St Cadoc's Home for Girls which at the time accommodated 200 children from the Monmouth Diocese. The aim was to rescue children who are left homeless, are cruelly treated or are in moral danger, and the society had 109 homes nationwide.

Newport Education Committee.

Silver Jubilee of His Majesty the King

The Newport Education Committee request the pleasure of
the company of

Mr. and Mrs. W. A. Gunn.

at a Mass Demonstration of Schoolchildren to be held at
The Newport Athletic Grounds,
on Monday the 6th May, 1935, commencing at
2.15 p.m.

An invitation to the mass demonstration of schoolchildren at Newport Athletic Club grounds in 1935. The invitation was addressed to the then Curator of the Museum and Art Gallery and his wife, Mr and Mrs W.A. Gunn.

The programme for a massed display on the Newport Athletic Club Grounds in celebration of the Silver Jubilee of King George V, 1935. There are children present from Newport high schools, secondary schools, the technical college, the junior instruction centres, central and elementary schools.

County Borough of Newport
EDUCATION COMMITTEE.

SILVER JUBILEE
of His Majesty The King,
1935.

Programme
OF
Mass Demonstration
OF
School Children
6th MAY, 1935.

At the
NEWPORT ATHLETIC GROUNDS
Commencing at 2.15 p.m.

A tea party celebrating the Silver Jubilee in 1935.

Newport Coronation Day Massed Parade in May 1937. The Mayor of Newport (Alderman I.C. Vincent) is reading the Coronation Proclamation of the new King George VI to the parade from the grandstand at the Newport Athletic Grounds. Also in the centre are the Dean of Monmouth, The Mayoress, Major J.E.C. Partridge, the Town Clerk and Lt-Col. A.Q. Archdale.

NEWPORT CORONATION CELEBRATIONS

✠   ✠

United

Coronation Service

NEWPORT ATHLETIC GROUNDS

Wednesday, May 12th, 1937
11 a.m.

ADMIT BEARER   **GRAND STAND**

An entrance card to the Coronation Service held at Newport Athletic Grounds in 1937.

Following the Coronation of King George VI in 1937, he and Queen Elizabeth, later HM the Queen Mother, visited Newport and here they can be seen driving through Maindee. This was the first time a reigning monarch and queen had made a visit to Newport and the town was highly decorated with bunting and flags for the occasion. It was during this visit that King George VI cut the first sod for the new civic centre. In Newport the Coronation had been celebrated with a week of organized events including a fête, a parade and a banquet.

A street party at Jenkins Street, Maindee, in May 1937, to celebrate the Coronation of King George VI.

Eight

Shops and Shopping

North's Butchers, Chepstow Road, Maindee, when it opened in 1918. It was owned by Mr John Hawkins of Whiston Road, Christchurch.

Woodgates baby carriages, Chepstow Road. The firm was established in 1905.

INVOICE

WOODGATES of NEWPORT LTD.
SPECIALISTS IN BABY CARRIAGES AND NURSERY NEEDS

3 & 4 Newport Arcade, High St.
Newport, Mon.
Tel. 58136

102 Chepstow Road
Newport, Mon.
Tel. 58134

M*rs* Horton.   16/10/58 19

Thurso, Wyndham St. Maches

1	Restmor toy Pram Green		6	19	6

Paid same time

Ello

Thanks

3580

J. Seary & Co., Printers, Newport, Mon.

A bill for a child's pram bought at Woodgate's baby carriages.

Maindee Square in 1959.

W. Thomas Ironmongers Ltd in 1965 with baby's pram and the company van outside.

For your Health's sake

buy the Best at

Telephone **2301**

Snowden's

L. W. G. SNOWDEN —————— **STORES**

RETAIL AND WHOLESALE

Grocers and Provision Merchants

18-20 Somerton Road, Newport, Mon.

OUR PRICES ARE KEEN AND COMPETITIVE, COMBINED
WITH A COURTEOUS AND EFFICIENT SERVICE

Advertisement for Snowden's stores, grocers and provision merchants based at Somerton Road.

Deccar General Stores on Caerleon Road in 1965 – a well-stocked hardware and ironmongers and decorators.

J.W. Watts general stores on Lliswerry Road in 1967, with a Woodbine cigarettes machine outside.

Garway Trading Company on Church Road in 1965, a well-stocked ironmongers and hardware dealers, with R. Neale's fish and chip shop on one side and Woolcot wool stores on the other.

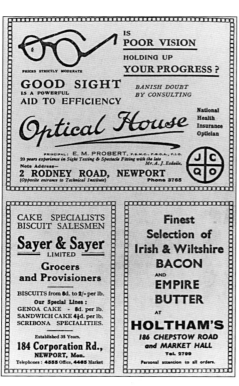

IS **POOR VISION** HOLDING UP **YOUR PROGRESS?**

PRICES STRICTLY MODERATE

GOOD SIGHT *BANISH DOUBT*
IS A POWERFUL *BY CONSULTING*
AID TO EFFICIENCY

Optical House

National
Health
Insurance
Optician

PRINCIPAL: E. M. PROBERT, F.S.M.C., F.B.O.A., F.I.O.
20 years experience in Sight Testing & Spectacle Fitting with the late
Mr. A. J. Esdaile.
Note Address—
2 RODNEY ROAD, NEWPORT
(Opposite entrance to Technical Institute) **Phone 3765**

CAKE SPECIALISTS
BISCUIT SALESMEN

Sayer & Sayer
LIMITED

**Grocers
and Provisioners**

BISCUITS from 8d. to 2/- per lb.
Our Special Lines :
GENOA CAKE - 8d. per lb.
SANDWICH CAKE 4½d. per lb.
SCRIBONA SPECIALITIES.

Established 35 Years.

184 Corporation Rd.,
NEWPORT, Mon.

Telephones : 4555 Office, 4465 Market

**Finest
Selection of
Irish & Wiltshire
BACON**
AND
**EMPIRE
BUTTER**
AT
HOLTHAM'S
186 CHEPSTOW ROAD
and MARKET HALL
Tel. 2799
Personal attention to all orders.

Various advertisements for retailers on the east side of Newport. They include cake specialists and biscuit salesmen on Corporation Road, an Optical House on Rodney Road, and a fine selection of Irish and Wiltshire bacon and empire butter at Holham's on Chepstow Road.

The corner of Rochester Road and Chepstow Road in 1965. Stedman's newsagent is on the left and J.E. Hodges on the right.

More advertisements for the east side of the river: gowns, suits and millinery, a chemist and a grocery store, all on Chepstow Road.

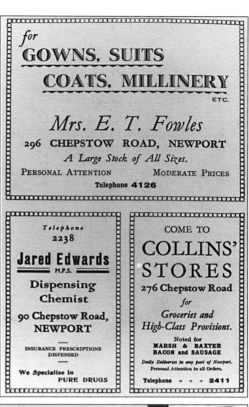

for
GOWNS, SUITS
COATS, MILLINERY
ETC.

Mrs. E. T. Fowles

296 CHEPSTOW ROAD, NEWPORT

A Large Stock of All Sizes.

PERSONAL ATTENTION · · · MODERATE PRICES

Telephone **4126**

Telephone
2238

Jared Edwards
M.P.S.

Dispensing Chemist

90 Chepstow Road, NEWPORT

—

INSURANCE PRESCRIPTIONS
DISPENSED

—

We Specialise in PURE DRUGS

COME TO
COLLINS'
STORES
276 Chepstow Road
for
Groceries and
High-Class Provisions.
Noted for
MARSH & BAXTER
BACON and SAUSAGE
Daily Deliveries to any part of Newport.
Personal Attention to all Orders.
Telephone - - - **2411**

Hardware stores on Chepstow Road in 1965.

Raleigh
THE ALL STEEL DEPENDABLE
CYCLE

For Comfort and Easy Running.

GUARANTEED FOR EVER.

from **£4 - 19 - 6**
or **2/2** Weekly.

Harry Stevens (Cycles) Ltd.
MAINDEE SQUARE

Telephone 3434.

Established 1899

Advertisement for Harry Stevens, cycle dealers in Maindee Square.

A bill from The Newport Mon. Machine-made Bread and Cake Manufactory in 1898. Their machine bakery was based in Caerleon Road.

Nine
Education

A pencil drawing by local artist W.J. Bush showing Eveswell School, Maindee, and surrounding houses before 1922.

The opening of Eveswell School on 4 February 1889. Miss Whitmarsh, headmistress, and her staff are shown outside. Miss Whitmarsh was the first headmistress of the school from 1889 to 1922. Eveswell had been opened to cater for the needs of newly developed areas and the overflow from Maindee.

A Merry Christmas from these girls in Eveswell School, c. 1900. In 1900 the school had to be enlarged due to the population increase in Maindee.

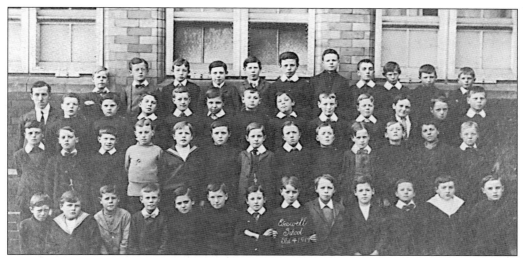

This group of boys and their master were part of Eveswell School in 1919.

The formidable-looking group pictured here made up the School Board in Newport in 1904. They would have been the education governing body, similar to local government education departments now. The first Newport School Board was formed in 1870 under the Elementary Education Act.

The opening of Newport Technical Institute on 29 September 1910. The Institute was opened by the Right Honourable Viscount Tredegar and became an excellent local Art College for students in and outside Wales.

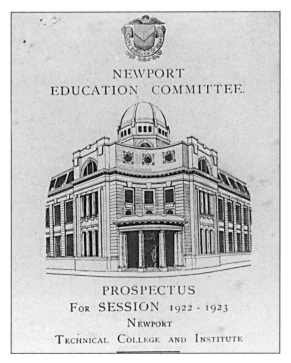

A prospectus for the Department of Arts and Crafts at Newport Technical College and Institute, for the session 1922-1923.

A view of Clarence Place, dominated by the impressive architecture of the Newport Technical Institute.

The boys of Church Road School in 1937.

Mr W.R. Lysaght, a local businessman, visiting Corporation Road Boys' School during the 1930s. Included in the photograph are: W.R. Lysaght, CBE, Desmond R. Lysaght, Councillor J.R. Wardell, Mr J.H. Roberts. Other members of school staff: B. Phillips, E.J. Dyer, W.R. Belgion, E. Coley, R.J. Jory, F. Godwin, F.S. Williams, E.H. Plumley, G.H. Newman, A.J. Watts, Miss E. Lloyd and Miss M. Burnett. Mr Lysaght is congratulating J.H. Roberts, the headmaster, for his thirty-eight years' service since the school had opened. Mr Roberts retired the following week.

Mr W.R. Lysaght returns to Corporation Road School for a tea to celebrate his eighty-first birthday on 11 March 1940. Mr Lysaght was presented with a birthday cake with eighty-one candles on it. Included in the group are, left to right around the cake: the Mayor of Newport (Alderman J.R. Wardell), the girl who presented the cake, Mr W.R. Lysaght, Mrs W.R. Lysaght, Mrs A. Higgins (the mayor's daughter).

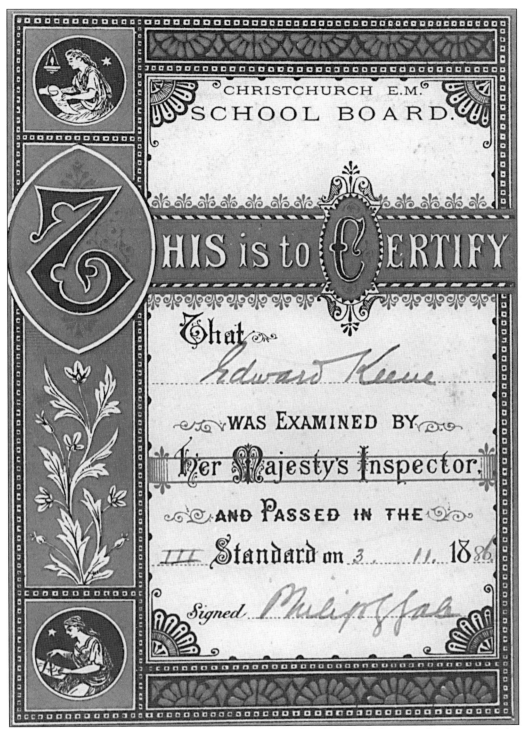

CHRISTCHURCH E.M.
SCHOOL BOARD.

THIS is to CERTIFY

That

Edward Keene

WAS EXAMINED BY

Her Majesty's Inspector,

AND PASSED IN THE

III Standard on 3 . 11 . 1886

Signed *Philip J Hall*

A certificate of education for Edward Keene of Christchurch School showing that he passed the Standard 3 school exam in 1886.

Church Road School children in Maindee in 1941. Church Road School was opened in 1881 and enlarged in 1928.

Maindee Junior School children in Chepstow Road, Maindee, in 1968. Members of St John the Evangelist Church in Maindee first met in 1864 to talk about the need for a school in the area. Six years later public elementary education was introduced as a result of the 1870 Education Act. One of the first established schools, Maindee opened in 1866 and, like Eveswell, it had to be enlarged in 1897 because of population increases.

The opening of Holy Cross Catholic School in 1936.

The laying of the foundation stone of the new St Julian's High School on 6 June 1939. Mr J.H. Williams, the contractor, presented the Mayor of Newport with a trowel for the ceremony. The County Borough of Newport, Monmouthshire Municipal Secondary School, formerly known as the Newport Higher Elementary School, moved from Stow Hill into this building on 30 June 1941. From that time onwards it became known as the Newport (St Julian's) High School.

The site of Alway School from the old quarry before it was built in 1948.

Alway School after it had been built, in 1959, viewed from the old quarry.

Ten
Sport and Leisure

Maindee Rugby Club, Cup winners in 1888/89. The first rugby ball ever seen in Newport was brought by the brothers William and Clifford Phillips in 1874, owners of Dock Road Brewery. Newport's first match was a draw against Glamorgan RFC at Cardiff. From left to right, back row: E.H. Teale (honourable secretary), R. Jenkins, R. Williams, Eli Evans, W.H. Watts, G. Hewitt, J. Howells (umpire), G.W. Antill (honourable secretary). Middle row: W. Groves, E. Lancaster, I.M. Johns, J. Osmond, W. Hunton, C. Hughes. Front row: F. Hunt, H. Jones, W. Jones, T. Pook.

In Newport, rugby has always been a popular sport, as can be seen in this photograph of the crowds returning to the west side of the river after a match at Rodney Parade. Newport Athletic Club was founded in 1875 and the first mention of the 'new ground' was in 1877 when the club was known as Newport Cricket, Athletic and Football Club.

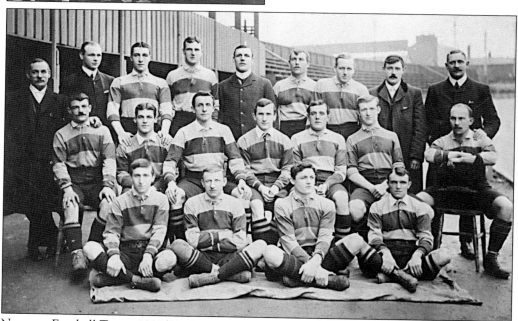

Newport Football Team, 1902/03. Newport Rugby Club gained a world-class reputation. There have been six occasions when they played a whole season without losing one match. From left to right, back row: G. Thomas (trainer), J.C. Jenkins, C.M. Pritchard, E.W. Gould, George Boots (vice captain), S. Adams, A.G. Brown, C.C. Pritchard, Harry Packer (touch judge). Second row: G. Spillane, C.E. Lewis, T.W. Pearson, G.I. Lloyd (captain), J.J. Hodges, G.H. Thomas, J.E.C. Partridge. Front row: C.L. Williams, D.J. Boots, E. Thomas, J. Hillman.

There has always been a strong international representation in Newport Rugby Club. Newport RFC has provided Wales with nearly 150 international players. All the International capped players were brought together for this group photograph in 1921. From left to right, back row: J.J. Hodges, T.W. Pearson, F. Parfitt, E. Jenkins, T.C. Graham, G. Travers, T. Pook, G.L. Hurst, E. Thomas, H. Wetter. Third row: E.G. Nicholls, H. Packer, P. Jones, T. Baker-Jones, H.S. Lyne, L. Attwell, J. Whitfield, A.W. Boucher, L. Trump, G. Boots, H. Dauncey. Second row: H. Uzzell, J. Wetter, R. Edwards, F.W. Birt, N. Macpherson, R.C.S. Plummer, P. Dibble, J. Shea, E. Hammett, D.E. Roche. Front row: A. Brown, P. Phillips, G. Thomas, W.J. Martin, C. Thomas, T.H. Vile, G.S.L. Lloyd.

The ladies of Colston Avenue Women's Football Team gathered for a match to celebrate the Coronation of Elizabeth II in 1953. From left to right, back row: Florrie Pask, Margaret Dukes, -?-, -?-, Barbara Donald, -?- (in background), Mrs Pearce, Iris Edwards, Mary Bassett, -?-, Mrs Lavender, Middle row: Doreen Edward, Ruth Daniels, Margaret Masterson, Iris Spruce, -?-, Margaret Daniels, Jeanne Donald. Front row: Mrs Spruce, Betty Dix, Olwen Dix.

Beechwood Bowling Club Tournament winning team in 1925 with their trophies. From left to right: H. Spicer (winner of Open Tournament, Abercarn), C.E. Budd (winner of Open Tournament, Brynawel) T. Johnson (winner of Open Tournament, Abergavenny).

Beechwood Bowling Club were also winners of the Newport Bowls League in the 1942/43 season. From left to right, back row: H. J. Sutton, E. Heyes, N.R. Grey, P. Bell, W.B. Hammett, T. Lewis, J. Clarke, E. Lewis, W.H. Baker, S. Hall, G.F. Jones, S. Clarke, W. Bateman. Front row: T. Whitehouse, W.E. Fry (honourable secretary), A.T. Bryant, (president), C.J. Plaisted (captain), A.H. Young, (chairman), W.F. Bell, F. Shellard.

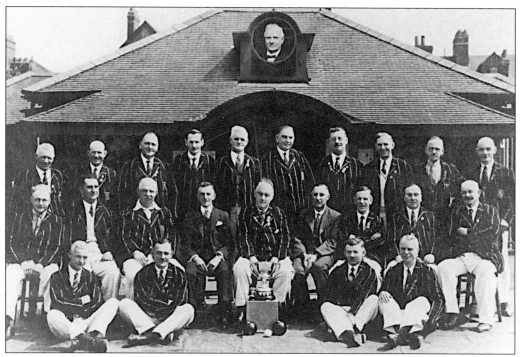

Newport Athletic Club also boasted a cup winning bowling squad. Here are the Private Green Champions of 1933. The Bowling Green had been laid in 1904 at a cost of £152; the official opening was in 1905 and the pavilion was built a few years later.

Lysaghts Amateur Football Club Team for the 1908/09 season.

Here are the Newport Cricket First XI in 1887. From left to right, back row: -?-, I. Wins, G.W. Taylor, Pritchard, A. Redwood (behind, in background) Clifford Phillips, F.J. Purdon, Butcher (groundsman). Middle row: J. Gould, Logan, F. Phillips, G Rosser, -?-. Front row: Killick (professional), Bob Gould, G.H. Gould (junior). There was a Cricket Club in Newport before 1850 but by the 1870s it seems to have disappeared. At this time another club, Victoria, was founded and was thought to be the nucleus of the cricket section of Newport Athletic Club. They played on ground now part of Shaftesbury Park, between Wyndham Street and Malpas Pill. The earliest known Captain of the First XI was Joseph Gould.

Newport County Football Club playing a match against Newport Cricket Teams in 1941/42.

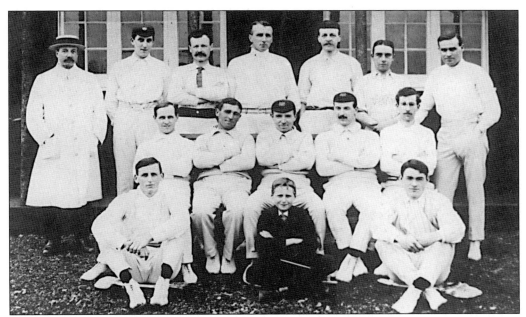

Maindee Thursdays Athletic Cricket Club XI in 1912. From left to right, back row: J.R. Jones (umpire), L.V. Pizzy (vice captain), R. Pullen, H. Clough, S. Myers, A.C. Williams, B. Nicholas. Middle row: W. Harries, T.H. Jones, H. Brown (captain), E.C. Cook (honourable secretary), A.E. Hannah. Front row: I. Lloyd, ? Pullen, E. Graham.

Blackberry picking at Christchurch at the turn of the twentieth century.

A view of the gardens of Beechwood Park, July 1939.

Beechwood Park and House which opened in 1900 to the public as a leisure facility. It was bought by the Borough Council for £11,500. In 1889 it had been sold at auction for £8,500 following the death of George Fothergill (mayor and tobacco importer) after the collapse of his family firm. He had originally bought the house for £18,000.

Members of the Simpson family at London Street, Maindee, *c.* 1946. The man is an Air Force cadet and the boy is a member of the Church Lads' Brigade. From left to right: John Simpson, Walter Simpson (a postman who was awarded the Imperial Service Medal), Margaret Simpson.

Orb Working Men's Club

NINETEENTH ANNUAL

Vegetable and Flower Show.

PATRONS:

President: Coun. A. E. Pugh, F.S.A.A., F.C.I.S., F.R.ECON.S.

Vice-Presidents:

His Worship the Mayor (Ald. J. R. Wardell), Ald. Major I. C. Vincent.
Capt. R. S. W. Harding, M C, J. B. Maddocks, Esq., T. Crowther, Esq.
G. Dix, Esq., Dr. Savage, Dr. Murphy, J. Davies, Esq., and other
Ladies and Gentlemen.

Chairman: Mr. J. DAVIES.

Committee: Messrs. E. Ashforth, J. Bell, J. Bird, T. Carless, J. Gordon
W. Clifford, D. Hubble, W. Jackson, W. Mason, C. Sellick, A. Davies,
G. Farrall, E. Lowe, H. Wesson.

Secretary: S. HOLLOWAY, 25 Hawthorne Avenue.

TO BE HELD AT THE

Orb Working Men's Club,

(JENKINS STREET), on

SATURDAY, AUG 26th, 1939.

Show to be Opened by His Worship the Mayor (Ald. J. R. Wardell),
at 2 p.m.

Judges: Messrs. Flynn and Shipp.

Schedules - 1d. each.

The cover of the programme for the Orb Working Men's Club Vegetable and Flower Show, August 1939. The show was held at the Orb Working Men's Club in Jenkins Street and opened by the mayor, Alderman J.R. Wardell.

The Coliseum Cinema showing the film *None Shall Escape*. The Coliseum Cinema in Corporation Road opened in early 1913. With the advent of television and competition from other cinemas, the Coliseum became two smaller theatres, known as Studios 1 and 2, in the 1970s. It eventually closed in 1987.

Staff from the Coliseum Cinema taking a break.

The Coliseum advertising car showing the week's movie attraction.

Eleven
Religion

Victoria Avenue Methodist church in 1893. The Newport Methodist Circuit was started in 1810; by 1867 the foundation stone was laid for a new Wesleyan Methodist Chapel at Maindee which was officially opened in 1868. It was intended to seat 300 people but plans were soon made to extend the building. In this illustration the church is shown after it had been much enlarged and could seat 925 people. In 1912 the coping at the front of the church was struck by lightning and some guttering and a decorative pinnacle fell off. There remained a crack down the building on the outer wall as evidence of this.

Wesleyan Preaching Room

MAINDEE.

SPECIAL SERVICES.

ON SUNDAY, JANUARY 19th, 1868, THE

REV. J. W. MARRIS

WILL PREACH AT 11 A.M., AND 6 P.M.;

Evening Subject :—" God's forbearance, and Man's abuse of it."

MONDAY, 20th,

A TEA will be provided, to commence at 5 o'clock, (admission by ticket), after which Addresses will be delivered by the Revs. E. SHELTON, J. W. MARRIS, and other Friends.

TUESDAY, 21st, THE

REV. J. W. MARRIS

WILL PREACH;

Subject :—" The Great Question."

WEDNESDAY, 22nd, THE

REV. J. B. BLANCH,

Subject :—" On Grieving the Holy Spirit."

THURSDAY, 23rd, THE

REV. E. SHELTON,

Subject :—Salvation—a word to the wise."

FRIDAY, 24th, THE

MR. F. H. ROBARTS,

Subject :—" The Invitation and Promise of the Gospel."

SUNDAY, 25th, THE

REV. E. SHELTON

WILL PREACH AT 11 A.M., AND 6 P.M.;

Evening Subject :—" Salvation—a word to the foolish."

THE WEEK EVENING SERVICES WILL COMMENCE AT 7 O'CLOCK.

ALL PERSONS ARE AFFECTIONATELY INVITED TO ATTEND.

G. F. PALMER, MACHINE PRINTER, STATIONER, ETC., MAINDEE.

A special services list for the Wesleyan Preaching Room which was probably situated over a grocer's shop owned by Thornes and at the rear of where the later Victoria Avenue Methodist church stood. It was probably used previously by a group of Baptists, before Summerhill Baptist church was formed. Summerhill Baptist chapel and Victoria Avenue Methodist church later had close links and the former had allowed the Victoria Avenue Methodist church to hold a meeting in their church on the day of laying the foundation stone.

Miss Mary Swinnerton presenting a bouquet to the Mayor of Newport, Councillor W.T. Griffiths, at the unveiling of a memorial tablet to the Revd James Swinnerton at the Newport Institute for the Blind and the Swinnerton Memorial Home. To the left of Miss Mary Swinnerton, the granddaughter of Revd James Swinnerton, stands the Bishop of Monmouth, Dr Joyce, and Mrs James Swinnerton is to the right of the mayor. The baskets in front of the group were made by the residents at Brook House. Rising costs and lack of support had forced the home at Llandevaud to close in 1918, but the work carried on in other buildings in Newport and eventually in 1929 the Blind Institute in Chepstow Road opened. Revd Swinnerton's own contribution by sponsoring the Brook House was not forgotten with the unveiling of the tablet where he is referred to as 'A Friend to the Blind'.

The staff of St John's Maindee, *c.* 1896. From left to right: Revd Howel Jenkins (later vicar of Glyncarwg), Revd Titmus, Revd James Swinnerton, Revd T.A. Davies (later vicar of Llanishen), Revd Cross. Revd James Swinnerton was vicar of St John the Evangelist, Maindee from 1889 to 1896. When he became vicar of Llandevaud in 1896, he devoted much of his time to the blind and during the summer many Maindee children would visit the Vicarage, Brook House, which was used as a residential home for the blind. The aim of the home was to provide a centre to co-ordinate work amongst the blind in the area and to be a place where Braille reading and writing, basket and mat making could be taught to blind adults. It also served as a holiday home as far as funds would permit. Classes and visits usually lasted two weeks, alternately for men and women, and they were taught by blind instructors.

St John's church, Maindee, destroyed by fire after an arson attack in 1949. St John's the Evangelist opened in 1870, after a small group met in 1858 in the King's Head Hotel to discuss the need for a church in Maindee which was still a rural area and part of the parish of Christchurch. The church was severely damaged as a result of the fire but the parishioners, together with the vicar, the Revd J.P. Stephens, raised money to restore it. During the First World War, 400 parishioners were lost and a memorial window is dedicated to them.

Summerhill Baptist Church Sunday School outing, *c.* 1890. Summerhill had been officially founded in 1862 with a group of seventeen members, who met in a rented upper room in Albert Avenue, many from the new housing estate at Fairoak. The church was officially opened in 1866 and was built on the site of the former orchard of Fair Oak Farm.

Summerhill Sunday School outing, c. 1890.

Right: Christchurch, Holy Trinity, after being severely damaged by fire through an arson attack in 1949. Christchurch was a vicarage for the priory of Goldcliff before it became the property of Eton College. The church existed in AD 1113 and the register dates from 1666. The parish included Maindee.

Below: Christchurch, Holy Trinity, in March 1959, following restoration after the arson attack in 1949. The church had also been restored in the nineteenth century and had reopened in 1886. The south doorway is Norman and the chancel dates from the thirteenth century. The aisle, outer walls, south porch, and high tower west of the south aisle are fifteenth-century. The chancel has an incised slab with figures of John and Isabella Colmer who died in 1376, known as the Healing Stone, which was said to have miraculous powers. The legend surrounding this stone said that if a sick person was laid on the stone overnight, they would be healed. There was dispute over which night was the most effective, although on the eve of Ascension Day in 1770, sixteen people were laid on it all night with the hope of being cured by the morning and in 1803 a healing service took place on the evening before Trinity Thursday.

This young girl, Hilda, aged thirteen, is in fancy dress for the Band of Hope Carnival in 1914. Photographed in Archibald Street, she is warning of the danger of 'intoxicants'.

Archibald Street Wesleyan Mission Concert in 1910. This was a Methodist Mission chapel of Victoria Avenue Church for the Eveswell area. At that time, they met on Sundays at 6.45 p.m., with Sister Sarah as their deaconess. The building was destroyed when a parachute mine fell in Eveswell Street on 1 July 1941, causing a large amount of destruction to the street and killing thirty-four people.

Archibald Street Mission Concert.

Archibald Street Wesleyan Mission Band of Hope Carnival on 4 July 1914. Hilda, the young girl pictured on page 112, is kneeling in the front row in her fancy dress.

Miss Joyce, the sister of the Bishop of Monmouth, laying the foundation stone for the new Sunday School at Somerton on 1 October 1936. The Bishop of Monmouth, who dedicated the building, stands on the left. The aim of the new Sunday School was to serve the needs of the Somerton Garden City district and it cost £3,300.

St Philip's church choir, c. 1950/51. St Philip's was a chapel of ease to St Andrew's church, Jenkins Street, Lliswerry. From left to right, back row: Tommy Horton, Cedric Jones, Gwyneth Frecker, Pat Roxborough, Maureen Newell, -?-, Don Felkin, John Davis. Middle row (left, behind): Glyn Thomas, Ken Rosier; (in front) ? Felkin, Graham Virgo, John Mitchell, Barbara Donald, Jean Miller, Jack Still (choirmaster), Barbara Jordan, Jackie Donald, John Gough, George Thorneycroft, Brian Banes (in front), Ivor Jarvis (with glasses). Unfortunately, the names of those on the front row are not known.

Choir Ecclesiastics at St Philip's church during the 1980s. The church of St Philip's was opened in 1925 and aimed to establish a congregation to develop the mission of St Andrew's. It was helped in this aim by Father Feetham and his assistants, the Church Army Officers and Sisters, and a loyal group of lay helpers. From left to right in the back row: Jack Still, Tyrone ?, Dilys Saunders, Rosemary Pearce, Mary Johnson. Middle row: ? Hancock, Jason Williams, Jonathan Fish, -?-, Yvonne Ritz, Caroline Fish. Front row: Revd Colin Wilcox, Revd Henry Davies, Revd Martin Cox.

Twelve
Urban Development

This aerial view of the East Bank of the Usk was taken in the early 1920s while construction of the new town bridge was in progress and before the completion of the Cenotaph. The athletic ground in the centre is laid out as tennis courts.

In 1900 when this photograph was taken, Crescent Road in Summer Hill was still semi-rural and right on the edge of the development to the east side of Newport. Beechwood Park is on the hill behind the terrace of houses.

Church House in Christchurch in 1900. This was undoubtedly the ancient manse of Christchurch, dating from the sixteenth century, adjoining the churchyard.

Between the wars, Lliswerry police station was set in a semi-rural landscape with a house and private gardens for the resident constable. It was demolished in 1936.

Bishpool Lane in 1945 was a quiet country lane. The roadway looks as if it needed some repair.

By 1949 street lighting had appeared on the scene and work had begun to clear the area on the right for the Bishpool and Treberth housing estate.

This is the view from Little Bishpool looking towards Ladyhill Wood, in 1953, before the building of the Alway estate.

Lliswerry Farm with signs of house building behind the farmhouse, 1946.

Lliswerry Farm buildings from the Lliswerry Road in 1945. In ten years, this part of town would change dramatically.

Seen from the same spot as the previous photograph, the changes are obvious here in 1955. The farm outbuilding closest to the camera has already been demolished and the rest of the old farm buildings would follow soon after.

In 1954, Elms Farm still stood in Lliswerry behind the trees that gave the farm its name. The housing development is already getting closer.

By 1959 only the telephone pole and some rubble remain to mark the site of Elms Farm.

Aberthaw Road in 1946 was still essentially open countryside with only a few houses visible on the hilltop.

By 1960 there were major building works in progress in Aberthaw Road, with preparation for a new roadway through the hillside.

In 1953 this was the site of the junction of Aberthaw Road and Ringland Circle as the Ringland Estate developed.

By 1960 there is a dramatic change in the scene. This is now the junction at Aberthaw Road and Ringland Circle on the Ringland Estate.

The end of Lliswerry Road, close to the then level crossing in 1954.

In Lliswerry Road the greenery also gave way to housing development as Newport's population grew.

Aerial view of the Ringland Estate, 1967.

Acknowledgements

With grateful thanks to the following people, without whose invaluable support and kind donations of images, this publication would not have been possible:

Glyn Bennett, Mike Bowers, Mrs Bowkett, Mr J.C. Burnes, Bruce Campbell, Roger Cucksey, Bill Davies, Alex Dawson, Mr and Mrs D. Galbraith, Mrs Goodwin, Mr Hughes, Ron Inglis, the family of Gwyn Jones, Mrs O'Keefe, Mr Powell, the friendly staff of the Reference Library, Graham Sadler, Miss Scott, Rachel Silverson, Mr and Mrs Simpson, *South Wales Argus*, *The Western Mail*, Mrs Irene Williams, Mrs Worthy, Dave Wyatt, all Museum and Heritage Service staff, and all those who over the years have kindly donated photographs to the collections of Newport Museum and Art Gallery.

Mrs Bowkett, a worker standing in front of an armaments poster inside the Royal Ordnance Factory, Wednesbury Street, during the Second World War.